PATSY'S GINGERBREAD FANTASY

poems by

Darlene M. Javar

Finishing Line Press
Georgetown, Kentucky

PATSY'S GINGERBREAD FANTASY

Copyright © 2025 by Darlene M. Javar
ISBN 979-8-88838-962-1 First Edition
All rights reserved under International and Pan-American Copyright Conventions. No part of this book may be reproduced in any manner whatsoever without written permission from the publisher, except in the case of brief quotations embodied in critical articles and reviews.

ACKNOWLEDGMENTS

Grateful Acknowledgment is made to the following publications in which these poems first appeared:

Bamboo Ridge Press: Journal of Hawai`i Literature and Arts ~ "Earthquakes, Tidal Waves and Tinfoil Barbs," "The Growing of Hope," "Love Travels Unconditionally," "Mom's Rules," "The Passing of Time," "Phonics, The Faye Nobody Tattoo Program," "Scavengers," "The Wake of Selective Memory"
Chaminade Literary Review ~ "Patsy's Gingerbread Fantasy," "A Yellow Tinge Wraps the Pile"
The Distillery ~ "Morning At Aunty's"
Earth's Daughters ~ "Works of Fire on New Year's Eve"
The East Hawai`i Observer ~ Dawn of the Widow
Into the Teeth of the Wind ~ "Conversation and Coffee at Mom's," "The Baking of Tradition"

Publisher: Leah Huete de Maines
Editor: Christen Kincaid
Cover Art: Darlene M. Javar
Author Photo: Kristin Wolfgang
Cover Design: Elizabeth Maines McCleavy

Order online: www.finishinglinepress.com
also available on amazon.com

Author inquiries and mail orders:
Finishing Line Press
PO Box 1626
Georgetown, Kentucky 40324
USA

Contents

- Patsy's Gingerbread Fantasy 1
- Phonics, The Faye Nobody Tattoo Program 2
- Earthquakes, Tidal Waves, and Tinfoil Barbs 3
- The Fishermom at Sunrise 4
- Morning at Aunty's 5
- Dawn of the Widow 6
- Conversing with Crustaceans 7
- Works of Fire on New Year's Eve 8
- The Growing of Hope 9
- Spectators 10
- Orchid Leis and Lies 11
- Resolve 12
- Mom's Rules 13
- Love Travels Unconditionally 14
- The Passing of Time 15
- Consolation Prizes and the Omnibus Budget
  Reconciliation Act 16
- The Wake of Selective Memory 17
- A Yellow Tinge Wraps the Pile 18
- The Baking of Tradition 19
- Scavengers 20
- Indian Giver 21
- Claws 22
- Nine Great-Great Grand Children and Now This Poem 23
- Conversation and Coffee at Mom's 24
- Notes 25

For my mother—
Patricia Bolos Torres,
and her grandchildren—
Amberly, Jessica, Greg Jr.

"*He pūnāwai kahe wale ke aloha.*
Love is a spring that flows freely.
Love is without bounds and exists for all."

#936 Olelo No'eau by Mary Kawena Pukui
Hawaiian Proverbs & Poetical Sayings

PATSY'S GINGERBREAD FANTASY

Patsy planned and built the fantasy
every caroling Christmas.
Rectangular sheets of sugar and flour,
leveled with caring hands,
lay hours in a hot oven.
A warm aroma of spice
sneaked out windows
of Patsy's kitchen.
Neighbors knew it was time again,
a holiday tradition—donation
to the Jaycees, Young Farmers or
Pāhala Library.
Powdered sugar icing cemented
candies of color and sweetness,
red licorice, M & M's, jellybeans,
orange jellied wedges, red and white
hard candy mints
onto the edible, incredible
gingerbread house.
Hungry eyes watched the assembly,
aching for a little taste of the dream.
The carpenter smiled, whispered,
"Doesn't it look delicious?"
before the final loving touch:
fumigation with a red can of Raid
to keep out the creepy critters
and little fingers of her own
Hansel and Gretel.

PHONICS, THE FAYE NOBODY TATTOO PROGRAM

Children learn
the letter F
from marks on Daddy's hand.

Which is it, Daddy?
Funny face,
flip flop,
five fingers?
Does FF really mean Fred Flintstone?

It's a fishy fish.

Children learn
silent e
from the name on Daddy's calf.

Who's Faye?
Why do the Y and E letters have to be quiet?
Mommy,
where's your name?
Aren't you his girlfriend too?

Fishy fish.

EARTHQUAKES, TIDAL WAVES, AND TINFOIL BARBS

I
The earth rocked. The ocean
sucked back. Local campers
scrambled in the dark
up the overgrown trail
through naupaka and a`a,
took sanctuary on the hill,
in the old Hawaiian church,
sentinel of the bay.
Moments later, two tsunamis
roared through Punalu`u Beach,
pavilions, campgrounds,
restaurants and homes.
Caught in the advancing sea,
swept inland,
gills of ulua, kala, and nenue
gasped in the rubble.

II
With every jolt,
Dad's sixteen aquariums rocked,
water splashing out—
three hundred gallons
spilling onto the floor,
flowing from the dining room,
through the hall,
into bath and bedrooms.
Tinfoil barbs, oscars, and tetra
thrashed in half empty tanks
as Dad and Mom waded
through ankle deep water
dragging a green hose
in from the back door,
through the kitchen, dining room,
into the first tank.
We huddled on the dining table—
broken glass and aftershocks.

THE FISHERMOM AT SUNRISE

As the tide rises, waves slide over the reef
like the knitted blanket she pulls over her first born
every cold evening, each crisp morning.
She stands on the shore alert
like a mother at the edge of a crib
studying the breath of her baby—
the chest rising, the chest falling;
swells, waves, crests, and valleys.
She bends slowly, one eye still on the ocean,
reaches for the rod and reel warmed by the sun.
Casting toward the flashing glimmer of scales,
she focuses on the orange floater bobbing,
her hook hidden beneath the morsel of shrimp.
Floater dipping under, the line tensing,
she grips the fishing rod
as if holding the hand of her children
threading through a crowd.

Scaled and gutted, oil hissing
like foam on the shore,
she fries the fish to feed her family
knowing she must caution her children—
watch for the bones.

MORNING AT AUNTY'S

Overnighter at Aunty's—
cable TV, Japanese dolls,
scooters, golf carts,
sounds of all night Hilo traffic,
was a glimpse of the world
outside Pāhala Plantation.
Resting on a handcrafted quilt,
pink stuffed terriers
in jewel studded collars never needed
to warn off unfriendly intruders.
Ruffled curtains bordered the window
easing in the glow of morning sun
warming figurines, and treasure-filled boxes.

Saturday morning
Mom gathered us around the quilt
to make the announcement—
facts she questioned at the hospital,
words she rehearsed in the car
traveling across Komohana Street,
the truth reverberating through Aunty's house
as she walked in the front door.

Daddy died this morning.

The sun kept shining as our world darkened;
four children wept from clouds of disbelief,
lifting the quilt to cover our pain.

Mother vowed,
we will survive, we will be strong,
yet she resembled a mattress
stripped of its cover,
abandoned at the dumpster.

DAWN OF THE WIDOW

She studies the curves
of his vinyl dining chair,
his place at the table—the best view
of the television across the room.
His lunch pail waits
on the floor by the refrigerator,
but she doesn't stoop to pick it up
this morning.
On the hook next to the kitchen door,
the metallic collection hangs—
car, locker, miscellaneous keys;
just outside on the porch steps—
steel toe boots.

With the mourning light, there is
no need to unlock the door,
no good-bye kiss,
no beginning
of a ten-hour shift.

CONVERSING WITH CRUSTACEANS

Where do you go
when the tide recedes
leaving your life barren and dry,
just a spray of salt to burn your eyes?
Where do you go
when the tide returns
your sandy walls caved in,
deluged by a tumble of waves?

Pat looks for answers in the tidepools,
trying to measure the currents
of her life, the ripples and waves
she endures, pulling her under;
every near drowning.

A crab pops out,
quickly scans his zone.
With sudden shifts of path
he makes his way
toward the water.

Mr. Crab,
don't you know
someday your shell
will dry out
and blow away with the wind?

No hesitation,
he plummets,
disappearing
into white foam.

WORKS OF FIRE ON NEW YEAR'S EVE

Her gas stove worked
all New Year's Eve Day—
sushi, shrimp,
crab tempura,
tombo-tombo,
mochi, suman,
noodles, rice.
Grandma Pat
had lots of food
for New Year's Eve,
not that she invited people,
but just in case they came.
Food to share
for a bright start,
an assortment of dishes
varied each year—
charsui, sweet sour ribs,
adobo, shoyu chicken;
along with soup
to take the chill off night's air—
watercress, miso,
Portuguese bean, or
chicken long rice.
Bottom fish for luck,
lucky Papa catch
onaga, ehu, paka,
wrapped in foil
steaming on the barbeque grill.
There were fireworks too
if you could get away
from the table.

THE GROWING OF HOPE

Removed from a highlighter,
the yellow felt tip immersed in water;
the plastic drinking cup,
latex gloves, straws, antiseptic wash
outlined Mom's private room basin.

The liquid too pale,
shell of the pen opened,
a longer cylinder of felt
brightened the shade.

Paper towels from a metal dispenser
were folded, added to the dye.
Sunshine absorbed,
dried under fluorescent lights,
the paper towels
were torn—
lengths of ragged edges—
were layered—
petal upon petal—
were gathered and twisted—
roses, carnations, hibiscus.

The quick dip of a blue felt pen tip
in the yellow mixture
created a subtle shade for greenery,
a lovely bouquet.

Borrowed from the nurse's station,
a roll of white tape fastened
the flowers into gardens of life
blooming on the bulletin board and wall.

With the minerals, vitamins, saline solution,
sunshine through glass windows,
the gardens kept growing
as Mom got better that particular season.

SPECTATORS

"One of the pigs is a runt. It's very small and weak, and it will never amount to anything. So your father has decided to do away with it."
"Do away with it?" shrieked Fern. "You mean kill it?"
    E.B. White, *Charlotte's Web*

Weakened by chemo and radiation,
her five-foot frame bedridden,
Mom silently watched
the spinning of the silken web—
Charlotte's glistening words
prolonging Wilbur's life,
the farm town gathering
to behold the radiant pig.

I watched Mom
view the animated version
of the literary classic,
and wondered
whether she identified
with the perpetual hope of a spider—
Charlotte's delicate miracles
hanging from rafters in a barn;
or if she sympathized
with Wilbur, trusting
in the help of Charlotte
and Templeton the Rat
who scurried
to find the right word
to make things better.

I pondered over
Mom's daily routine,
her impassive expression,
the video rewound, rewatched;
Charlotte's life force fading,
Charlotte dying;
Wilbur's animated immortality.

ORCHID LEIS AND LIES

She wanted an orchid garden—
Hawaiian cattleyas, lavender vanda;
wanted to see her children and grandchildren grow,
kept reassuring them, "I'll be home soon."

She wanted an orchid garden—
'okika honohono, and enough blooms to make a lei;
to lay beneath her Hawaiian orchid quilt
and wake up to the aroma of fresh Ka`ū Coffee.

She wanted an orchid garden since her 51st birthday
when we bought her orchids, later promising
we'd water them, and they'd be waiting
in her patio; purple orchids of perpetual bloom.

Final days of wanting— orchids moved to the ICU,
I slept on the floor near the elevator, near other people
with the same expression—
people waiting for people wanting orchid gardens.

I went back to her old floor where her nurses
gave me a towel, a pillow, and another lie
as I entered the empty waiting room to sleep on the couch,
"Everything is going to be alright."

RESOLVE

At fifty-two
she said she could
live with the tubes,
tests, medication,
needles and probes
in a convalescent home
among the gray and weary,
blind and bedridden,
the paralyzed and forgotten.
She could live
with the picc line, fistula,
and bags of earth colored residue
and be satisfied.

MOM'S RULES

Over the months, each day
we took a breath,
postured our hearts
before turning into room 222,
always in compliance
with her rules:
Be strong. Don't cry.

The decisive procedure
wasn't just another
can't-see-she's-going-to-make-it,
call-the-family surgery.
Nurses wheeled that body
back from surgery, its blood
draining into plastic bags and cylinders
at each side of its jet-black head,
at each side of its swollen torso,
at each motionless foot,
between its grotesque legs—
spatter on white sheets.
Then she had the nerve
to open her knowing eyes
so we couldn't cry.

LOVE TRAVELS UNCONDITIONALLY
For Rodney

Get out
if you can't handle it,
conditional love
for her lover, friend,
fishing partner, pond builder, welder,
mechanic, sparring partner, victim
of nineteen years.
He wanted to marry her.
She wanted to marry him.
Never in the same breath
until it was too late.
He drove one hundred ten miles,
round trip, Pāhala-Hilo-Pāhala,
to that hospital on the hill
every day, one hundred days,
eleven thousand bittersweet miles.
Then he took a plane
every week
to Oʻahu, Queen's Medical Center,
to massage her legs,
wipe her mouth,
hold her hand,
love her unconditionally.

Last trip, last words.
She whispered,
Get out!
He left to cry
next to the nurses' station,
tears controlled within seconds
knowing they would
never see each other again
in this life.

Go home.

THE PASSING OF TIME

Respirator removed,
tubes unplugged and pushed aside,
we gathered, prayed,
said our goodbyes, kissed Mom's cheeks,
and watched the monitor and her chest
move in the slowest, most deliberate way—
rising, pausing,
lowering, pausing.

Twenty minutes later
we continued to witness
every slow draw of breath,
each cleansing exhale,
and we knew
she was taunting us,
making monkey face,
sticking out her tongue,
winking her eye
one last time.

The sun went down
and we began to get comfortable,
chat about the weather,
stroke her leg,
hold her hand,
write poetry.

We kept the all-night vigil,
then met the new day,
but morning faded into noon,
forcing us to accept
that time belonged to her
and she would linger
as long as she damn well pleased.

CONSOLATION PRIZES AND THE OMNIBUS BUDGET RECONCILIATION ACT

Young widow, four children—
*"Social Security
will take care of the family.
Money for college,"*
consolation prizes Dad's
coworkers lamented.

Financial deficits,
the Feds defaulting,
children worked in the fields
to supplement income—
no one foresaw the scaling-back
or elimination of expenditures—
college students.

Nineteen years later, Social Security
revisited, mom collected
the booby prize—
disability for disease
and the side effects of radiation.

Plantation workers returned
for her funeral remembering Dad
and those same four children
reappearing
on the first pew.

THE WAKE OF SELECTIVE MEMORY

I choose to not remember her
as cadaver; hard marbled mass
beneath the resemblance of skin,
painted, polished, powdered,
the mortician taking great pride
in the near replica of a pocket-sized picture.
I choose to not remember her body
lying motionless in a satin lined box,
ruffled and stitched to perfection,
velvet trimmed with edges of silver.
I've erased from memory
the placement of hands resting
from the work of daily living,
forgotten the feel
of my lips to her forehead,
the sound of no good-bye
calling out to me as she leaves
in a polished blue hearse.

A YELLOW TINGE WRAPS THE PILE

Seven months of unread memories,
your year's subscribed Hawai`i Tribune,
forwarded to my box,
wait stacked in the corner of my dusty garage.
Obsolete headlines, proclamations of the moment,
weather away like the forecast,
cloudy, with a chance of rain.
A yellow tinge wraps the pile
of international summits,
train wrecks, hurricane warnings,
NBA championships, and
corporate mergers.
No mention of you.
You once had a baby blue house
surrounded with roses,
chickens scratching up the backyard,
green tabis drying on the clothesline,
a karaoke voice flowing through Keahi Street.
Ka`ū Agribusiness pay stubs,
Good Housekeeping subscriptions,
Finger Hut orders are canceled.
Newspaper for training puppies,
starting fires, lining drawers, stuffing boxes,
saving dishes, wrapping fish,
cleaning windows, making kites,
remind me of how life moves on
without you.

THE BAKING OF TRADITION

I
In the closet, on the bottom shelf,
beneath the dust and dark layers
of Mom's stored belongings,
treasured tattered cookbooks—
black and white composition tablets
of Christmas, Easter, rainy day surprises
are discovered. Memories grow
like pineapple upside down cake in her oven.
Daughters sit in the hallway
savoring scents of cinnamon,
nutmeg, turmeric, anise
on Betty Crocker books,
Time Life International Cookbooks,
and magazine clipped creations.
Rabbit recipes hop about the laughter.
Tradition and holiday flavor
rise out of books sparkling like glass ornaments
hanging from a Christmas tree.
Leafing through pages,
pausing at check marks,
mouths watering at double-checked items,
stomachs gurgling at recipes tripled and quadrupled,
pounds build around our waists,
knowing she added ingredients,
remembering she measured by eye.

II
My children and I bake bread—
speckled with raisins, sprinkled with cinnamon,
braided, and glazed with confectioners sugar.

SCAVENGERS

When you are dead
it is easy for others
to touch up
your photo albums
and paint a new portrait
of the you
they have transformed,
quote your words
and thoughts
to their benefit,
rearrange your heirlooms
into slabs of furniture,
resurrect your remains,
restructure your skeleton
so you no longer
have a backbone,
claim "best friends"
to entitle them—
a place of honor
beside the latest
memory of you.
These successors
redefine your essence,
recycle your goods,
pick at your body
as if you can't
look them in the eye.

INDIAN GIVER

I demand
your
Mother's Day bath robe,
knotted love earrings,
and Christmas jewelry box
as if worldly possessions
crystallize your spirit.

I take back homemade
gifts from the heart,
thoughts that count,
and the gold
that doesn't glitter
in your limelight
anymore.

CLAWS

You search with hawk-like eyes
for anything
bright, shiny, valuable
to place in your nest,
                your nest,
your very own precious nest.

I'd like to take
the delicate speckled eggs
from your nest,
smash them against
twigs and twine,
watch the yellow yolk,
translucent slime,
run down, discolor your bright,
shiny, valuable everythings.

SIX GREAT-GREAT-GRANDCHILDREN AND NOW THIS POEM

Learned your mother passed,
was going to call you
but didn't.

Read condolence messages,
was going to write to your brother
but didn't.

Well, could've left a message once
on voicemail
but you know the outcome.

Double checked her obituary,
changed my clothes, got in the car,
but never started the engine.

Was going to contact my niece
who works for your sister
to tell her to tell your family

that I'm thinking of her
almost obsessively,
but I don't do goodbye.

I picture your parents,
Uncle Bobby and Aunty Phoebe,
three decades ago, in my parents'

garage after my mom's funeral
the same place they sat drinking coffee
in Styrofoam cups two decades prior

following my dad's February funeral,
your mom being last,
my dad being first in death among friends.

CONVERSATION AND COFFEE AT MOM'S

When the gray sky hangs like a ceiling,
rain shimmering like chandelier crystals,

I want to drive up to Mom's,
have a cup of coffee, fresh pastries, or bread,

the warmth of her oven eliminating the need
for sweaters and wool socks.

Conversation and quiet moments
would flow like rain on the roof

falling in the right places to water
miniature roses, simple pleasures, and needs.

But she doesn't live up the road anymore;
cookie sheets remain in the cupboard.

Cookbooks placed in a brown paper bag
are delivered to my home

because maybe I could use them.
Perhaps, if the afternoon rain subsides, I could

visit my mother-in-law;
she's a mother,

and she likes conversation,
quiet moments, and coffee.

Notes

Patsy's Gingerbread Fantasy
- Pāhala /Pa-ha-la/ A rural town on the Big Island of Hawai`i. Originally a sugar plantation town.

Earthquakes, Tidal Waves, and Tinfoil Barbs
- naupaka /now-pa-ka/ A Hawaiian shrub with 'half-flowers', one variation found near the ocean and another variation found in the mountains. Hawaiian legend express that the flowers are separated lovers.
- a`a /ah-AH/ Lava that is rough and jagged.
- Punalu`u /poo-ne-loo-oo/
- ulua /oo-loo-wa/ A popular sport/food fish caught off Hawaiian shores.
- kala /ka-la/ A Hawaiian fish usually caught through reef spear fishing.
- nenue /nay-noo-ee/ A popular sport/food gray chub that lives on or near the coastline.

Morning at Aunty's
- Hilo /hee-lo/ A town on the northeastern side of the "Big Island" of Hawai`i.
- Pāhala /Pa-ha-la/ A rural town on the southeastern side of the "Big Island" of Hawai`i.
- Komohana /ko-mo-ha-na/ (Street) A street that passes approximately north-south through the town of Hilo.

Works of Fire on New Year's Eve
- tombo-tombo A Filipino desert made with mochiko balls in a sweet coconut milk sauce.
- mochi /mo-chee/ A Japanese dessert made with glutinous rice flour, symbolic of good luck and auspiciousness.
- suman / soo-mahn/ A Filipino dessert made with glutinous rice flour, sugar, and coconut milk, wrapped in banana or coconut leaves.
- char siu /char-shu/ A Cantonese red barbeque/roast pork dish, sweet and spicy.

- adobo /ah-doe-bo/ A Filipino meat or fish dish cooked with vinegar, garlic, and soy sauce.
- miso /mee-so/ A Japanese fermented soybean paste used to make soup, or for seasoning
- onaga /o-na-ga/ Long tail Hawaiian Red Snapper, bottom fish popular for New Years and other celebrations.
- ehu /eh-hoo/ Short tail Red Snapper, bottom fish popular for New Years and other celebrations.
- Paka (Opakapaka) /o-pa-ka-pa-ka/ A pink snapper, bottom fish popular for New Years and other celebrations.

The Growing of Hope
- hibiscus /hi-bis-cus/ A large shrub with large blooms and very thin petals, with many variations of bloom color and type.

Orchid Leis and Lies
- ʻokika honohono /oh-kee-kah ho-no-ho-no/ A dendrobium, a species of the orchid.
- Kaʻū /ka-oo/ The southern and largest district on the "Big Island" of Hawaiʻi.

Love Travels Unconditionally
- Pāhala /Pa-ha-la/ A rural town on the Big Island of Hawaiʻi. Originally a sugar plantation town.
- Hilo /hee-lo/ A town on the northeastern side of the "Big Island" of Hawaiʻi.

A Yellow Tinge Wraps the Pile
- tabis /ta-bees/ A Japanese shoe where the big toe is separated from the rest, made of cloth and a slip resistant bottom, usually worn at the beach.
- Keahi /Kay-ah-hee/ (Street) The name of a street in Pāhala Town.
- Kaʻū /ka-oo/ The southern and largest district on the "Big Island" of Hawaiʻi.

Darlene M. Javar is a trans-Pacific and interisland commuting baby-sitting grandmother. When she's not on a plane or with her mo'opuna, she could be picking coffee, fishing, quilting or tending her roses. Her poems are published by *Bamboo Ridge Press, Chaminade Literary Review, Hawai`i Pacific Review, Into the Teeth of the Wind, The Distillery, Earth's Daughters, Storyboard 8, Kaimana, Tinfish,* and *East Hawai`i Observer.* Her poetry is recorded in "Rural Voices Radio II," National Writing Project, and "Aloha Shorts", a co-production of Hawai`i Public Radio and Bamboo Ridge Press. Her work is also cited in *The Bloomsbury Handbook of Contemporary American Poetry* (Svonkin and Axelrod, 2023).

www.ingramcontent.com/pod-product-compliance
Lightning Source LLC
Chambersburg PA
CBHW022059080426
42734CB00009B/1421